BRAIN BOOSTERS

By Sidney Martin and Dana McMillan
Illustrated by Corbin Hillam

Publisher: Roberta Suid
Editor: Elizabeth Russell
Cover Design: David Hale
Design and Production: Susan Pinkerton
Cover Art: Corbin Hillam

ISBN 0-912107-43-X

Printed in the United States of America

9 8 7 6 5 4 3 2 1

Contents

Introduction

Brain Boosters presents games and activities to stimulate original, inventive thinking in children. Designed for teachers and parents, *Brain Boosters* is packed with ideas to help children develop problem-solving skills. Each project in the book provides opportunities for logical thought, from construction steps through rules of play.

The project materials are simple, inexpensive, and easy to find. Check the resource page at the end of the book for help in locating the raw materials to collect before beginning a project. In many cases, different materials may be substituted, adding to the creativity of the project.

The games and activities in this book can be used simply as described at home or in the classroom. In many settings, the challenge of making the game is as much fun as playing it with a friend. These projects are an excellent way to use time on a rainy day at home or when work has been completed in the classroom.

Some of the activities in *Brain Boosters* have been used in student problem-solving workshops held at The Learning Exchange, a nonprofit educational resource center. These workshops were developed to meet needs expressed by parents and teachers in the metropolitan Kansas City area. See the description of the Jet Car for an example of turning a design activity into a challenge that stretches analytical thinking skills.

Many *Brain Boosters* projects can be expanded into challenge activities in the classroom for a group of students. Follow this general format to make maximum use of the ideas.

1. Collect needed materials.
2. Present basic construction steps from the book.
3. Allow time to create the project.
4. Play a trial game.
5. Write directions for play based on the trial game.
6. Play the game again and make revisions as necessary.
7. Set up challenge teams among students.
8. Report and graph the results.
9. Hold a group meeting to review the process and results.

Some of the projects make particularly good gifts. Older students can make the Bead Puzzle, for example, as a present for a younger child. Children will enjoy stumping their parents with the Hanoi Tower.

However you use *Brain Boosters*, we hope your results match the results of those who visit The Learning Exchange each year: challenging adventures in problem-solving.

Sidney Martin and
Dana McMillan
The Learning Exchange, Inc.
2721 Walnut
Kansas City, MO 64111

Tri-Peg Jump

Try to remove all the nails except one in this strategy game.

MATERIALS:
Copy of diagram
Tri-wall cardboard triangle, 6 ¾″ on each side
14 small nails
1 large nail
Colored markers

CONSTRUCTION:
1. Place the copy of the diagram on the cardboard and mark the 15 dots with a pencil.
2. Make a hole at each dot with a hammer and the large nail.
3. Decorate the triangle with the colored markers.
4. Place the 14 small nails in the holes, leaving one hole empty.

RULES OF PLAY:
1. Jump one nail over another into an empty space. This is the only type of move allowed. Remove the jumped nail.
2. Continue jumping and removing nails until no other moves are possible. Try to have only one nail left.

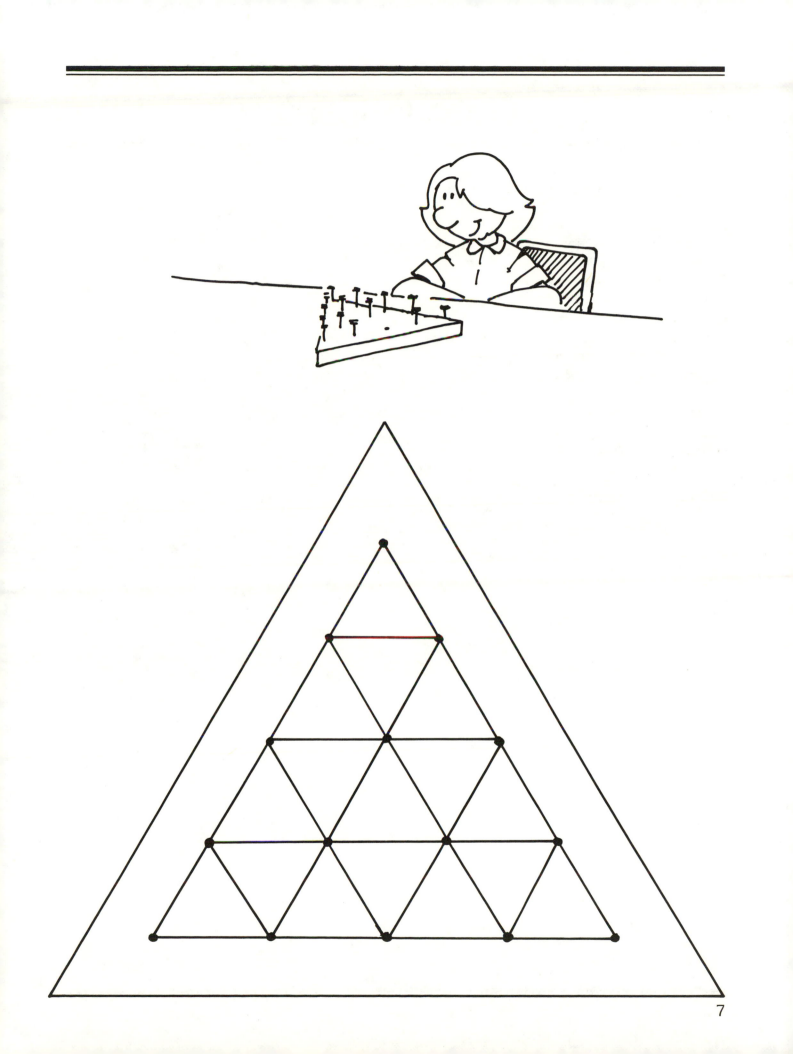

Betcha Can't

Use logic to arrange shape and color cards in this game.

MATERIALS:
4 sheets of construction paper (red, yellow, blue, green)
Envelope or zip lock bag
Small card (optional)

CONSTRUCTION:
1. Cut a circle, a square, a rectangle, and a triangle from each of the four colors of construction paper.
2. Print the name of the game and the directions on the envelope or on a small card.
3. Store shapes and directions in the envelope or bag.

RULES OF PLAY:
1. Arrange the 16 shapes in four rows of four so that no shape or color is repeated in any row.
2. There must be four different shapes and four different colors in each vertical, horizontal, and diagonal row.

Tic-tac-toe

Make simple tic-tac-toe sets for quiet play.

MATERIALS:
4 popsicle sticks
White glue
12 beans, 6 of one kind and 6 of another
Small zip lock bag
Index card

CONSTRUCTION:
1. Place two sticks parallel to each other about 1½" apart.
2. Glue the other sticks at right angles to the first two. Allow to dry.
3. Print the name of the game and the directions on the index card and store it in the zip lock bag with the sticks and the beans.

RULES OF PLAY:
1. Each player takes six beans.
2. Players take turns placing a bean in one of the nine grid sections.
3. Play continues until one player has three beans in a row diagonally, horizontally, or vertically — a tic-tac-toe.

3-D Tic-tac-toe

This version adds an extra dimension to the original game.

MATERIALS:
Copy of the pattern
4 strips of tri-wall cardboard, 6" x 1½"
3 plexiglass squares, 3¾" x 3¾"
Ruler
Fine-point permanent marker
Utility knife
White glue
40 beans (20 each of two different kinds)
Index card
Zip lock bag

CONSTRUCTION:
1. Place each plexiglass square over the pattern. Draw the grid, using the ruler and fine-point marker.
2. Mark the four tri-wall strips as shown.
3. Cut a deep slit at each mark with the utility knife.
4. Put a small amount of glue on the corner of one plexiglass square and insert it into a slit on the cardboard. Repeat with the other two plexiglass squares.
5. Attach the other three legs, one by one, using the same method.
6. Print directions on the index card and store it in the zip lock bag with the beans.

RULES OF PLAY:
1. Each player gets 20 beans of the same kind.
2. Players take turns placing one bean on any of the 27 squares.
3. The game is won when one player has three beans in a row, horizontally, vertically, or diagonally, on one plane or through all three.

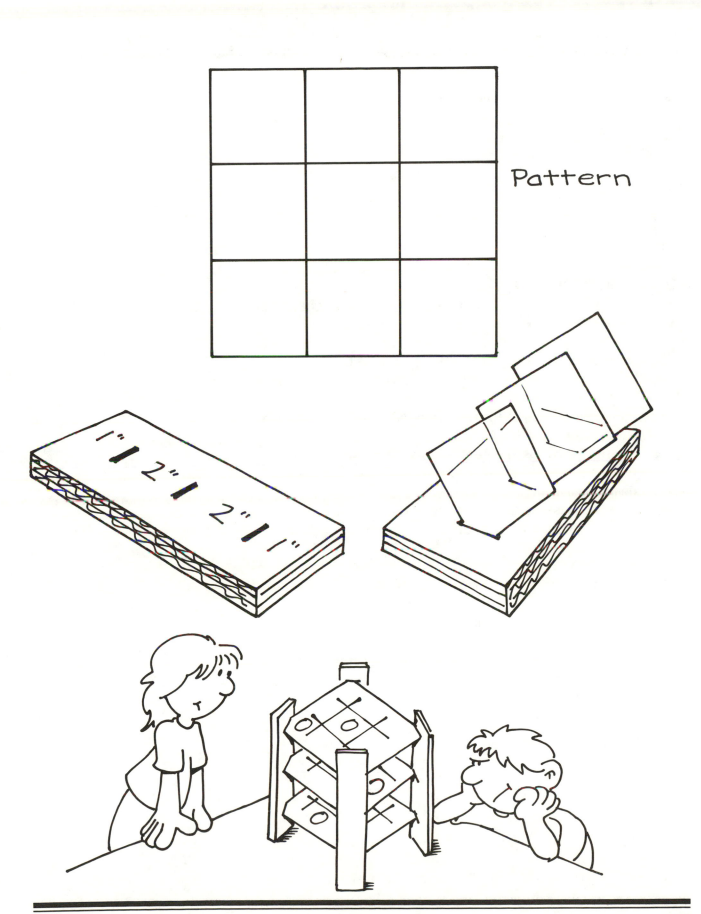

Pattern

Hanoi Tower

Improve logical thinking powers with this game.

MATERIALS:
Tri-wall cardboard base (4″ x 12″)
6 cardboard squares (1½″, 2″, 2½″, 3″, 3½″, 4″)
3 wooden dowels (3″ long, ⅛″ diameter)
1 large nail
White glue
Colored markers

CONSTRUCTION:
1. Draw a line lengthwise along the center of the cardboard base. Mark the location of the dowels on this line at 2″, 6″, and 10″ from one end.
2. Make three holes in the base with the large nail.
3. Dip the end of each dowel into white glue and insert it into one of the holes.
4. Stack the six squares to form a tower, with the largest square on the bottom.
5. Punch a hole through the center of this stack with the nail.
6. Widen the holes with a pencil to help them slip onto the dowels easily.
7. Decorate the base and squares with the colored markers.
8. Stack the squares in a tower on one of the end dowels.

RULES OF PLAY:
1. Move the tower from one dowel to another.
2. Never put a larger square on a smaller square.
3. Move only one square at a time.

Hint: Start with a tower of three squares and learn to move it. Then make the game more challenging by adding squares, using what you have learned.

Egg Cup Fill-Up

Use strategy and addition facts to win this game.

MATERIALS:
Egg carton without lid for each set
Cardboard base, 10" x 12", for each set
White glue
1 egg cup for each set
2 dice
12 beans for each set

CONSTRUCTION:
1. Glue the egg carton to the cardboard base.
2. Glue the egg cup to the lower right corner of the base.
3. Print the name of the game and the directions on the base.
4. Number the 12 cups as shown.
5. Place the 12 beans in the extra cup.
6. Make two or more sets of this game.

RULES OF PLAY:
1. Two players take turns rolling the dice and putting a bean in the cup or cups that equal the number rolled. Example: Roll a 6 and a 3; put a bean in 9 or beans in 5 and 4.
2. Play continues until one player fills all the cups. If all players are stumped, add up each player's empty cups. Low score wins.

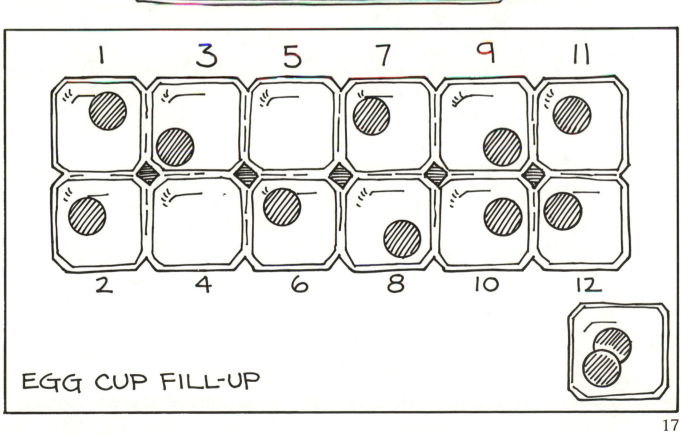

EGG CUP FILL-UP

Egg Carton Multiplication

Make a complete set to practice all the multiplication facts.

MATERIALS:
1 egg carton for each multiplication table
1 bean for each egg carton
Permanent markers

CONSTRUCTION:
1. Number the cups in the carton from 1 to 12, using permanent markers.
2. Print the number to be multiplied inside the lid.
3. Place the bean inside the egg carton and close the lid.
4. Print the answer for each cup on the bottom of the egg carton to make this activity self-checking.

RULES OF PLAY:
1. Shake the carton. Open the lid to see what cup the bean is in.
2. Multiply the number written on the lid by the number in the cup.
3. Score by adding each correct product.

Division Board

Demonstrate division and remainders with this board.

MATERIALS:
11 egg cartons
Cardboard base, 22″ x 22″
110 beans
White glue
Index cards
Small zip lock bag

CONSTRUCTION:
1. Cut the lids off the egg cartons.
2. Cut one egg carton in half lengthwise.
3. Cut two cups off the ends of five egg cartons.
4. Glue the egg cartons to the base in rows, 11 cups across and 11 cups down.
5. Number the cartons as illustrated.
6. Write division problems on index cards. Store cards and beans in zip lock bag.

RULES OF PLAY:
1. Read one division problem card. Example: $37 \div 6 = 6$, remainder 1.
2. Count out enough beans to match the divisor. Example: 6. Place these beans in the divisor cups.
3. Count out enough beans to match the dividend. Example: 37. Place these beans in the rows under the filled divisor cups.
4. The answer is the number of filled rows plus the remainder.

$$37 \div 6 =$$

divisor →							7	8	9	10
1										
2										
3										
4										
5										
answer → 6										
7										
8										
9										
10										

Magic Square

Make all the rows add up to the same number.

MATERIALS:
Cardboard base, 9″ x 9″
1½″ egg cartons
Envelope
16 paper disks

CONSTRUCTION:
1. Cut the egg cups apart and glue them to the base in rows of four across and four down.
2. Pick a magic number. This can be any number.
3. Mark the magic square combinations on the paper disks. These are addends, four of which will total the magic number. Example: 30 = 6, 14, 7, 3, 3, 1, 6, 20, 7, 12, 6, 5, 14, 3, 11, 2.
4. Mark the magic number on the envelope and store the 16 paper disks inside.

RULES OF PLAY:
1. Put one disk in each cup.
2. Arrange numbers so that each horizontal and vertical row adds up to the magic number.

Simple Balance

Place different objects in the cups to see which is heavier.

MATERIALS:
Quart or half-gallon milk carton
Sand
Cardboard strip, 1" x 12"
String
Brad
2 small styrofoam cups
Beans, macaroni, shells, and other materials to weigh

CONSTRUCTION:
1. Cut off the top of the milk carton. Place sand inside to weight it down.
2. Punch a small hole in the exact center of one side of the milk carton near the top.
3. Punch a hole at the exact center of the cardboard strip. Then punch a hole at each end of the strip the same distance from the center.
4. Attach the cardboard strip to the carton with the brad.
5. Punch two holes through the top of each cup. Attach the cups to the strip of cardboard with string. Make sure the cups hang evenly.

USES:
1. Experiment to find two different objects that have the same weight according to the balance.
2. Put beans in one cup and dry macaroni in another. Keep adding, one at a time, until the cups balance.

Finger Balance

Conduct a balancing act with this simple project.

MATERIALS:
Bottle cork, 2″ diameter
Nail
2 small knitting needles

CONSTRUCTION:
1. Poke the nail into the center of the wide end of the cork.
2. Carefully push a knitting needle into each side of the cork near the narrow end.

USES:
1. Balance the nail on your finger.
2. Try using knitting needles of a different size to see if the cork will still balance as well.

Kalah

Play this centuries-old game from Africa and Asia.

MATERIALS:
Cardboard egg carton
36 beans
Stapler

CONSTRUCTION:
1. Remove the lid from the egg carton and cut it in half crosswise.
2. Measure 2″ in from outside edge of each lid and draw a line. Cut away all but this 2″ of the bottom of each lid, leaving the brim intact.
3. Fold in the side pieces and staple to form the Kalah dishes.
4. Staple a Kalah dish to each end of the egg carton.
5. Place three beans in each of the 12 egg cups.

RULES OF PLAY:
1. Two players sit on opposite sides of the board. Each player tries to accumulate as many beans as possible in the Kalah dish to his or her right.
2. Each player in turn picks up all the beans in any one of his own six cups and puts them one by one in each cup around to his right. If there are enough beans to go beyond a player's Kalah dish, they are distributed in the opponent's cups, except for the opponent's Kalah dish.
3. If the player's last bean lands in his own Kalah dish, he or she gets another turn. If the last bean lands in an empty cup on the player's side, the player captures all of his opponent's beans in the opposite cup and puts them in his own Kalah dish together with the capturing bean. A capture ends the move.
4. The round is over when all six cups on one side are empty. The other player adds the remaining beans in his or her cups to the Kalah dish to the right. The player with the most beans wins.

FOLD ENDS IN

PLAYER b

b1   b2   b3   b4   b5   b6

K
A
L
A
H

b

a

K
A
L
A
H

a1   a2   a3   a4   a5   a6

PLAYER a

Mystery Pendulum

Demonstrate a kind of mind reading with this gadget.

MATERIALS:
2' of string
Washer or other small metal object

CONSTRUCTION:
1. Slip the string through the washer or tie it to the small metal object.
2. Tie the ends of the string to make a long loop.

RULES OF PLAY:
1. The mystery pendulum answers questions.
2. Hold one end of the string between the thumb and forefinger so that the washer is suspended just above another person's palm.
3. Think of a question. Ask it aloud and watch the pendulum. Don't try to make the pendulum swing. Concentrate on the question and the pendulum will begin to swing on its own. Thought creates a physical reaction. Thinking about the question causes the pendulum to move.
4. A back and forth motion indicates "yes," and a circular motion means "no."

Three Men in a Boat

Try to reverse the red and yellow men in this game of logic.

MATERIALS:
Tri-wall cardboard base, 2" x 8"
6 dowels, 2" long
Nail
Colored markers

CONSTRUCTION:
1. Mark off seven evenly spaced dots in a row on the cardboard.
2. Make a hole with the nail at each dot.
3. Widen the holes with a pencil so that the dowels will fit into them easily.
4. Color three dowels yellow and three dowels red.
5. Decorate the base with colored markers.

RULES OF PLAY:
1. Place the yellow men in three spaces at one end and the red men in three spaces at the other end. Leave the middle space empty.
2. Try to reverse the positions of the red and yellow men.
3. Move men forward only, never backward.
4. A man may move into the neighboring space, or if that space is occupied, he may jump over it.

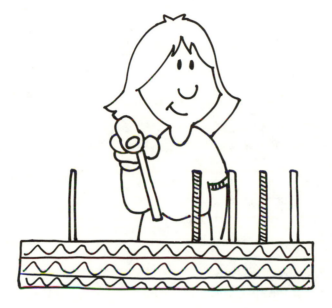

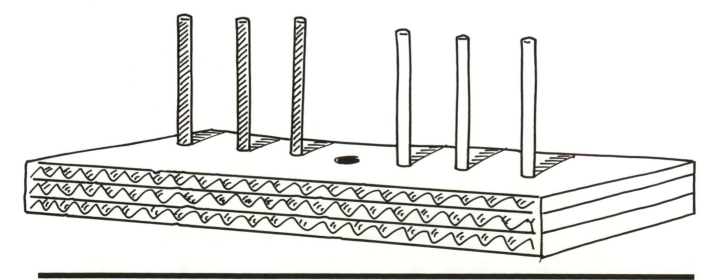

Thaumatrope

Fool the eye into believing an elephant can live in a bird cage!

MATERIALS:
Copy of the patterns
2 large, sturdy rubber bands
Posterboard
Colored markers or crayons
White glue

CONSTRUCTION:
1. Color the patterns with markers or crayons.
2. Cut out the patterns and mount on the cardboard with white glue, matching tops.
3. Trim the cardboard to the circular shape of the patterns.
4. Punch a hole in each side where indicated.
5. Slip one end of the loop through the other and pull tight.

USE:
1. Hook an index finger through each rubber band.
2. Twist the rubber bands tightly between thumbs and index fingers to turn the circle.
3. Release the thumbs and watch as the circle twirls quickly.
4. The elephant appears to be in the bird cage. A phenomenon called "continuity of vision" makes the two pictures look like one.

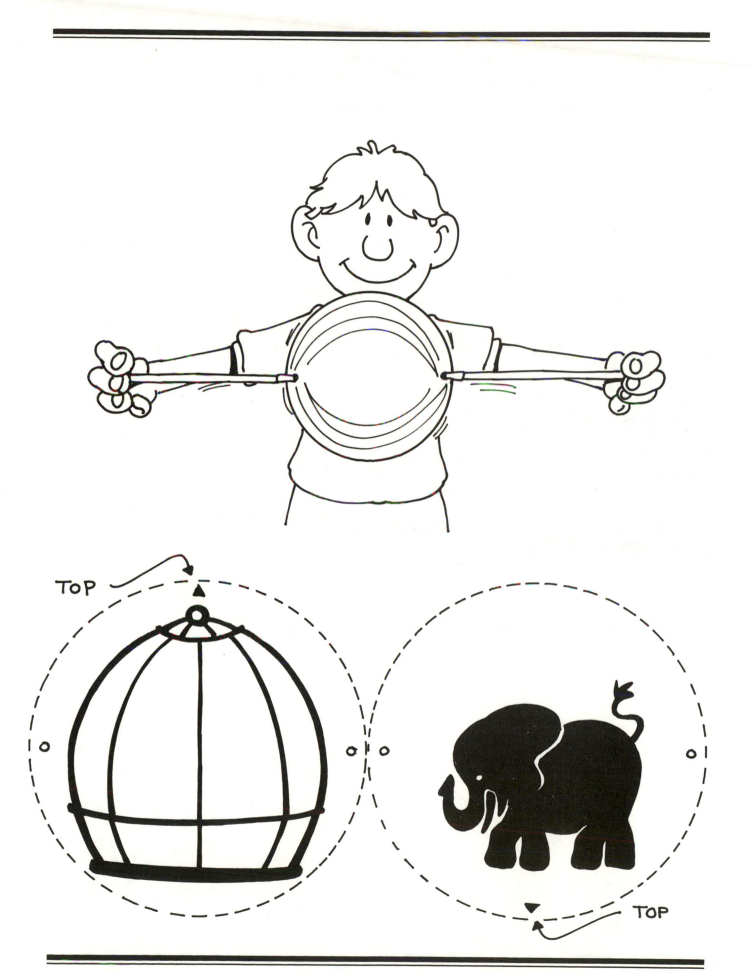

TOP

TOP

Circuit Tester

Light up the bulb with a complete circuit.

MATERIALS:
1½-volt flashlight battery
Margarine container with lid
Flashlight bulb
Flashlight receptacle
Two 24" lengths of telephone wire
Newspaper
Masking tape

CONSTRUCTION:
1. Strip about one inch of insulation from each wire end.
2. Attach a wire to the side contact of the receptacle.
3. Screw the bulb into the receptacle. Tape the receptacle to the top center pole of the battery.
4. Tape a second wire to the bottom of the battery.
5. Place the battery and receptacle in the margarine container. Make a hole in the plastic lid for the bulb and two smaller holes for the wires.
6. Use crumpled newspaper to hold the battery up against the lid.
7. Touch the wires together. The bulb should light up if the connections are good.

USE:
1. Use this circuit tester with the circuit board on the following pages to make a quiz game.
2. The bulb will light when the answer is right.

1½-volt flash-light battery

Newspaper crumbled in the box

Circuit Board

Watch the circuit tester light up when items match correctly.

MATERIALS:
12″ x 18″ sheet of construction paper
6″ x 12″ sheet of paper
2 paper clips
10 strips of aluminum foil, ½″ wide
Masking tape

CONSTRUCTION:
1. Draw boxes on the 6″ x 12″ paper as illustrated to make a quiz sheet. Leave 2″ at the top and make ten rows, 1″ apart.
2. Fold the 12″ x 18″ construction paper in half and paper clip the quiz sheet on the front.
3. Punch holes in the construction paper next to the small boxes.
4. Open the construction paper and randomly connect the holes on the left to the holes on the right with strips of foil. (Ignore the holes in the back half.)
5. Cover these foil strip circuits with masking tape.
6. Refold the construction paper to hide the circuits.
7. Fill in the boxes on the quiz sheet with questions and answers, placing pairs according to the circuit connections on the inside. Examples: words and definitions, math problems and answers, states and capitals, dates and events.

USE:
1. Take a wire in each hand.
2. Find a matching question and answer on the quiz sheet.
3. Touch one wire to the hole in the circuit board beside each fact.
4. If the bulb lights up, the answer is correct. If not, try another answer.

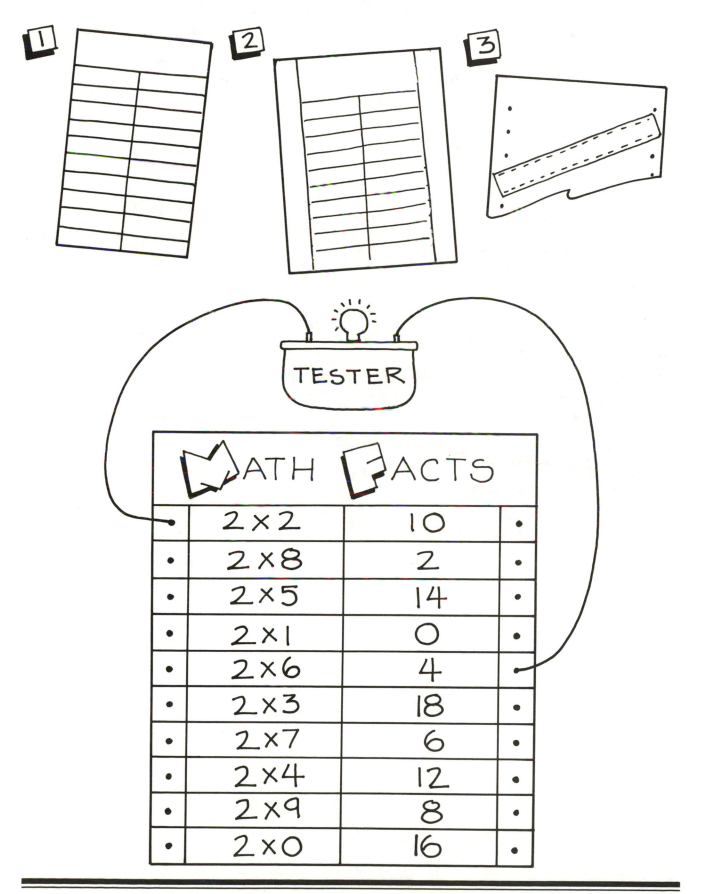

1

2

3

TESTER

MATH FACTS

2 x 2	10
2 x 8	2
2 x 5	14
2 x 1	0
2 x 6	4
2 x 3	18
2 x 7	6
2 x 4	12
2 x 9	8
2 x 0	16

Home Movie

Use simple sequence drawings to make your own movie.

MATERIALS:
12″ cardboard circle
10″ paper circle
Large nail
Rubber cement

CONSTRUCTION:
1. Cut narrow slits about 2″ apart and 2″ deep along the outer edge of the cardboard circle.
2. Center the paper circle on the cardboard circle and glue it on with rubber cement.
3. Draw a series of pictures around the edge of the paper circle. Draw one picture beneath each cardboard tab between the slits. Simple line drawings work best.
4. Poke the nail through the center of the circle so that the end comes out the back. Widen the hole slightly so that the wheel spins freely. Use the nail end as a handle.

USE:
1. Try out the device by looking into the mirror through the slots. Spin the wheel and watch what happens.
2. Make sequence drawings on additional paper circles, if desired, and change circles for a new movie.

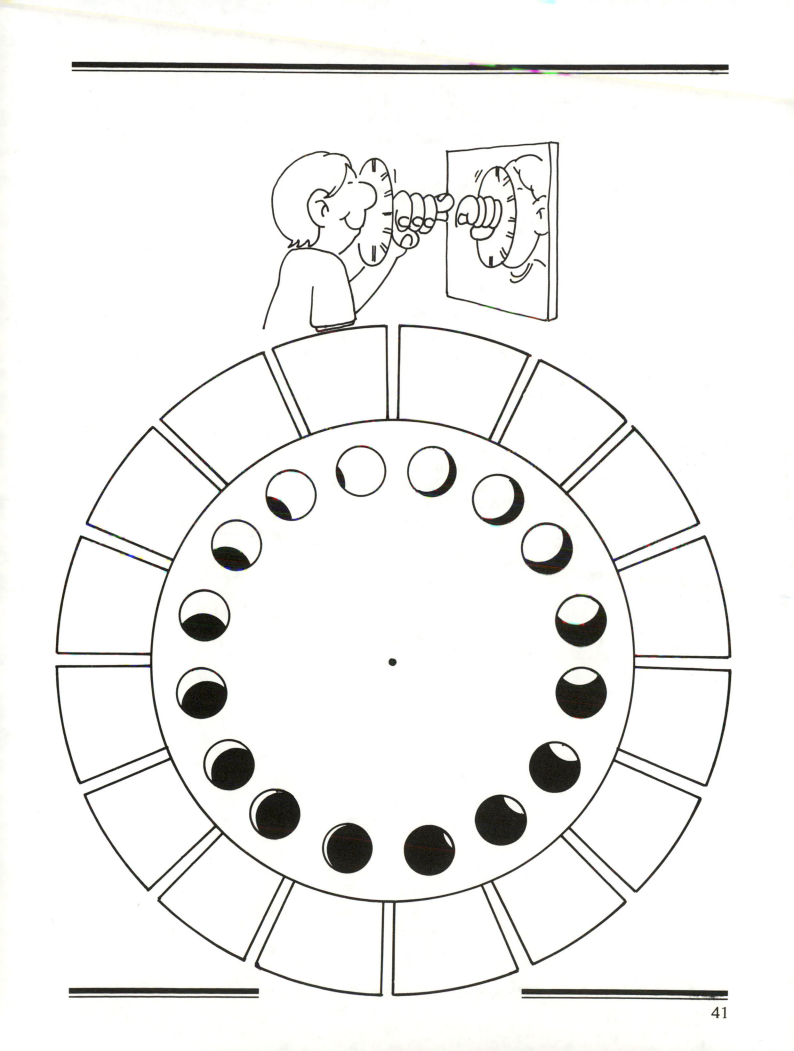

Capital Concentration

Learn states and their capitals with this memory game.

MATERIALS:
101 index cards, 3″ x 5″
Colored marker
Envelope or zip lock bag

CONSTRUCTION:
1. Print the name of a state or capital on each index card.
2. Print the name of the game and directions for play on the last index card.
3. Store all cards in the envelope or zip lock bag.

RULES OF PLAY:
1. One, two, or three students may play.
2. Players mix up the cards and lay them all face down.
3. The first player turns over two cards. If they match, the player keeps them and gets another turn. If they do not match, the player returns them to the same positions, face down.
4. Play continues to the left. Each player turns over two cards, one at a time, trying to match pairs.
5. When all cards have been matched, the player with the most pairs wins.

OTHER USES:
1. Start playing this game with only 10 or 15 pair of cards, then increase gradually to all 50 states and capitals.
2. Play concentration with cards prepared with number facts, synonyms, antonyms, definitions, science facts, dates and events, or any other set of questions and answers.

BOSTON

TALLAHASSEE

HELENA

DENVER

AUSTIN

SACRAMENTO

SPRINGFIELD

CALIFORNIA

ILLINOIS

FLORIDA

TEXAS

COLORADO

MONTANA

MASSACHUSETTS

43

Jet Car

This balloon-powered car can travel 20 feet or more.

MATERIALS:
2" x 2" x 5" box
9" balloon
2 drinking straws (2½" long)
Drinking straw (4" long)
2 wooden dowels (3" long, ⅛" diameter)
4 bottle caps
2 rubber bands
Masking tape
Hammer
Small nail

CONSTRUCTION:
1. Tape the two short straws on the bottom of the box to house the dowel axles.
2. Make a small hole in the center of each bottle cap wheel with the hammer and nail.
3. Force one wheel onto each axle. Wheels should fit tightly.
4. Put each axle through a straw on the box bottom and attach the other two wheels.
5. Insert the long straw section into the neck of the balloon about ¾". Secure with a rubber band.
6. Poke holes in the box so that the straw can be mounted at an angle aiming toward the floor. Secure with a rubber band.

USE:
1. Blow through the straw to inflate the balloon, pinching off the straw to trap the air.
2. Set the car on the floor and let it go.

Jet Car Challenge

Organize a problem-solving activity around building jet cars.

MATERIALS:
See "Jet Car" description. Provide a variety of body and wheel materials (boxes, tubes, egg cartons, plastic and metal lids), enough for each individual or small team.

CONSTRUCTION:
1. Describe the principle of a jet car to the class. Show how a balloon's energy can be harnessed by attaching the balloon to a straw. Demonstrate several wheel and body materials. Show how straw sections can house axles and reduce friction.
2. Divide the class into small teams. Have teams meet to design, construct, and name their cars.
3. Allow teams to test their cars during the construction phase.
4. Make a chart to record the distance traveled by each car.

USE:
1. Mark off a track with masking tape on a smooth floor.
2. Measure the distance each car travels and record it. After each team has had a trial run, allow time for the teams to make design revisions that will improve performance.
3. Hold a second run and record the distances.
4. Follow up with a discussion of the design improvements. Graph the results.

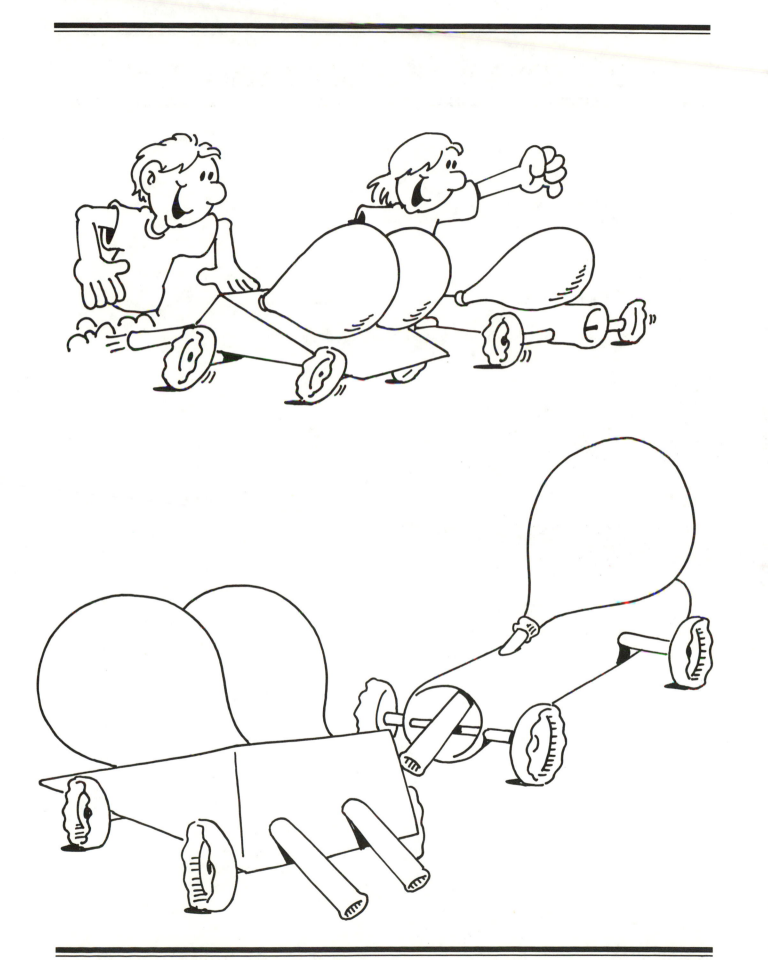

Styrofoam Cup Computer

Check multiplication skills with this project.

MATERIALS:
2 styrofoam cups with wide lips
Fine-point permanent marker

CONSTRUCTION:
1. Place one cup inside the other.
2. Write the multiplication table for one number on the outer cup.
Example: 1 x 6, 2 x 6, 3 x 6, etc.
3. Write the answers spaced to match the problems on the lip of
the inside cup.

USE:
1. Make a set of two cups for each of the multiplication tables.
2. Mix up the cups and challenge students to put them all
together correctly.

2×6 = 12
3×6 = 18
4×6 = 24
5×6 = 30
6×6 = 36

2×5 = 10
3×5 = 15
4×5 = 20
5×5 = 25
6×5 = 30

The Last Straw

Two can play this addition and subtraction game.

MATERIALS:
2 strips of tri-wall cardboard, 1" x 12"
Permanent marker
24 small nails
Hammer
Straws that will fit over the nail heads
2 dice

CONSTRUCTION:
1. Number each cardboard strip from 1 to 12 along the bottom edge.
2. Pound a nail above each number.
3. Cut the straws into 1" segments and place a segment on each nail.

RULES OF PLAY:
1. Each player uses one gameboard. Players take turns rolling the dice to make addition or subtraction problems. Example: A roll of 6 and 2 can be 6 + 2 or 6 − 2.
2. The player who rolled the dice decides which problem to use and computes the answer, removing the straw above that number on the board.
3. If a player cannot remove a straw, the turn is passed.
4. Play continues until one player removes all the straws on the gameboard, winning the game.

1 2 3 4 5 6 7 8 9 10 11 12

Bead Puzzle

Test eye-hand coordination with this game.

MATERIALS:
5" cardboard circle
4 cardboard rings, 5" diameter
5" circle of clear acetate
Picture from a greeting card
Glue
6 small beads
Decorative paper (optional)
Yarn

CONSTRUCTION:
1. Frame the picture with one of the cardboard rings and draw around the outside. Cut out the picture and glue it onto the cardboard circle.
2. Glue three cardboard rings onto the circle, one on top of another. Reserve the fourth ring.
3. Poke six small holes in the picture. Place the beads on the picture and try them in the holes, making any needed adjustments.
4. Glue the acetate circle onto the top cardboard ring.
5. Cover the remaining cardboard ring with decorative paper, if desired. Then glue the ring onto the acetate circle.
6. Glue yarn around the edges to finish.

USE:
Gently tilt the puzzle back and forth until each bead rests in a hole.

YARN

Braille Game

Learn the Braille alphabet while playing a game.

MATERIALS:
Braille alphabet chart
26 cards cut 2″ x 3″
Hole punch
Zip lock bag

CONSTRUCTION:
1. Use the Braille alphabet chart to determine the placement of dots at the top of each card.
2. Punch out the dots with the hole punch.
3. Print the letter on the back of each card.

RULES OF PLAY:
1. Two players sit facing each other. Between them is the deck of cards, front side up.
2. One player draws a card and shows the front of it to the other player. The second player must identify the letter. If correct, the second player keeps that card. If incorrect, the card goes to the bottom of the deck to be played again.
3. Players take turns showing and identifying letters. The winner names the most letters correctly.

OTHER USES:
1. Players follow basic rules above, but put on a blindfold and identify letters by touch, rather than by sight.
2. Make 36 cards, one of each consonant and three of each vowel. Deal out all cards to two players. Players take turns laying down cards to make words until one player runs out of cards. Award one point for three- or four-letter words, two points for five-letter words, three points for words with six or more letters.

a	b	c	d	e	f	g	h	i	j

k	l	m	n	o	p	q	r	s	t

u	v	w	x	y	z	capital sign	numeral sign

The Graphing Game

Two players chart their moves on a grid to determine the winner.

MATERIALS:
12" x 12" posterboard
Markers
Ruler
36 pennies
Small zip lock bag
Pair of dice

CONSTRUCTION:
1. Draw the gameboard on one side of the posterboard as illustrated, using markers and ruler.
2. Print these directions on the back of the gameboard:

> Divide the pennies between the players and decide who will use heads and who will use tails.
> Highest roll of the dice goes first.
> Each player rolls the dice and places a penny on the correct dot to show the outcome. Example: 6 and 3 could be row 6, column 3 or row 3, column 6.
> First player to cover all dots in any vertical, horizontal, or diagonal row wins the game.

3. Store pennies and dice in zip lock bag.

USE:
Players must use logic to determine which of two possible moves will best increase their chances of completing a row.

THE GRAPHING GAME

Game of Squares

A homemade geoboard provides a challenging game of squares.

MATERIALS:
Copy of the pattern
6" x 6" tri-wall cardboard square
25 small nails
40 small rubber bands (20 red, 20 blue)
White glue

CONSTRUCTION:
1. Cut out the pattern.
2. Place the pattern on the cardboard square. Mark the dots on the cardboard with a pencil.
3. Remove the pattern.
4. Dip the nails in white glue and press one in at each dot. Allow the glue to dry.

RULES OF PLAY:
1. Two players choose a color and sort the rubber bands.
2. Players take turns placing one line segment on the board by looping a rubber band around two nails.
3. Players receive one point and an extra turn upon completing a square.
4. When all possible squares have been made, the player with the most points wins.

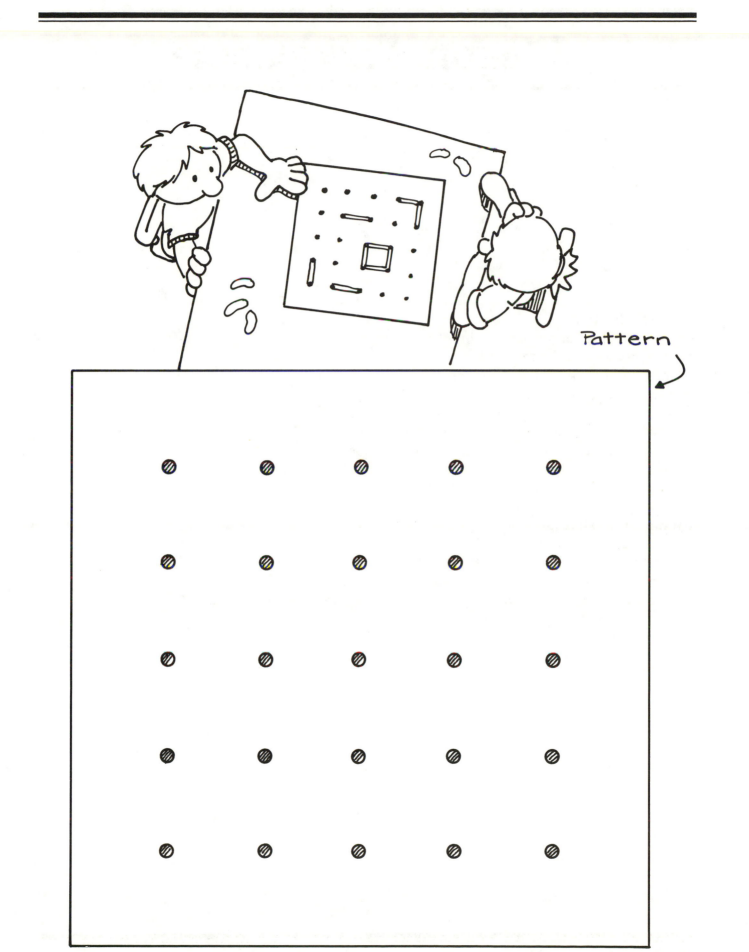

Pattern

Wagon Wheel Game

Two can play this strategy game.

MATERIALS:
2 paper plates
Stapler
Marker
9 bottle caps
8 beans (4 light, 4 dark)
String

CONSTRUCTION:
1. Cut a small section from the rim of one plate. Staple the two plates together, face to face.
2. Glue the flat sides of the bottle caps onto the plate. Draw the connecting lines as shown.
3. Place the beans in the bottle caps, arranged as shown.
4. Punch two holes in the open section of plate rim. Thread string through the holes and tie to make a loop for hanging up the game.
5. Store beans inside the plates when not in use.

RULES OF PLAY:
1. Players choose a color and decide who will go first.
2. A player must move to the empty bottle cap without jumping over any other bean. Players take turns moving.
3. A player cannot move a bean to the center space unless that bean is next to a bean of another color.
4. There can never be more than one bean in a bottle cap.
5. The object of the game is to block the other player and prevent any moves.

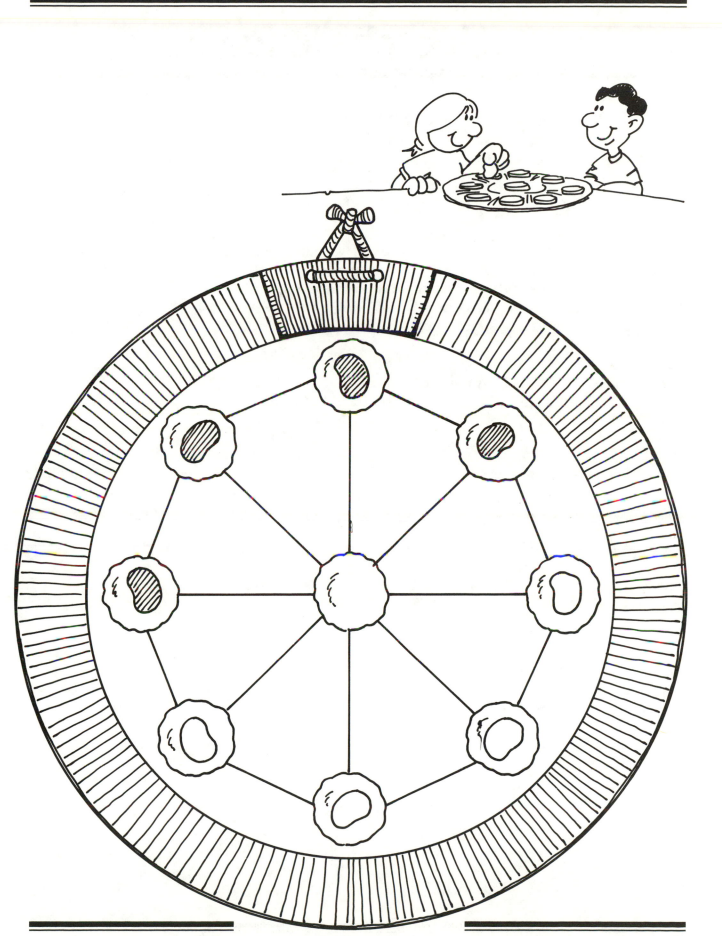

Geo-challenge

Create a variety of geometric models with this activity.

MATERIALS:
Paper clips
Drinking straws

CONSTRUCTION:
1. Link paper clips as shown. It is possible to link two, three, or four paper clips to make a joint.
2. Slip a straw over the end of each paper clip to create a side.
3. Continue to add links in the same way.
4. To make a cube, use 12 straws and 24 paper clips.

USES:
1. Try to make a triangular pyramid and other shapes or solids.
2. Make up a formula to show the number of straws and paper clips.

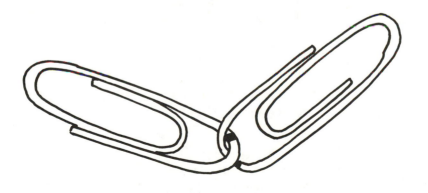

Resources

HOUSEHOLD DISCARDS:
craft sticks
single wall cardboard
egg cartons
*dice
milk cartons
bottle corks
margarine containers
small boxes
bottle caps
**tri-wall cardboard
telephone wire

VARIETY OR DIME STORE:
construction paper
paper
index cards
knitting needles
rubber bands
yarn
posterboard
paper clips
brass paper fasteners
9″ balloons

HARDWARE STORE:
nails
wooden dowels
flashlight batteries
flashlight bulbs, receptacles
string
plexiglass

GROCERY STORE:
zip lock bags
dried beans
styrofoam cups
aluminum foil
drinking straws
paper plates

EQUIPMENT NEEDED:
hammer
markers
white glue
rubber cement
hole punch
scissors

utility knife
pencil
ruler
stapler and staples
masking tape

*Make dice by cutting cubes from large styrofoam packing pieces with a band saw. Make the dots on each face with a marker.

**Make tri-wall cardboard by spreading a thin layer of glue on two sheets of single-wall cardboard. Sandwich together with a third sheet, clamp or weight, and let dry.